C000127744

WATCHMAN NEE

NEW BELIEVER'S SERIES

CONSECRATION

Living Stream Ministry
Anaheim, California

7

First Edition, November 1997.

ISBN 1-57593-963-0

Published by

Living Stream Ministry
2431 W. La Palma Ave., Anaheim, CA 92801 U.S.A.
P. O. Box 2121, Anaheim, CA 92814 U.S.A.

Printed in the United States of America

02   03   04   05   /   10   9   8   7   6   5   4   3

CONSECRATION

Scripture Reading: Exo. 28:1-2, 40-41; 29:1-25; Lev. 8:14-28; Rom. 6:13, 16, 19; 12:1; 1 Cor. 6:19-20; 2 Cor. 5:14-15

Let us now turn to the matter of Christian consecration.

Whether or not a person consecrates himself depends on whether he has a healthy salvation experience. If he views his faith in the Lord Jesus as being a favor to the Lord and his faith in God as a courtesy to Him, it will be impossible to talk to him about consecration. It is equally futile to talk about consecration to a person who feels that he is promoting the cause of Christianity and that his conversion is a great honor to it. Such a one does not have a good start in his Christian faith; he does not have a good beginning. It is impossible to expect him to consecrate himself. We must realize that it is the Lord who has graced us and granted mercy to us. It is the Lord who loves us and has saved us. This is why we consecrate our all to Him.

Teaching concerning consecration can be found in both the Old Testament and New Testament. Many passages in the New Testament, such as Romans 6 and 12, speak of consecration. In the Old Testament consecration is spoken of with special reference to Aaron and his household. Exodus 28 and 29 and Leviticus 8 speak of the consecration of Aaron and his household. Although consecration is the first basic experience of our service to God, we do not find many direct teachings from God's Word concerning it. In order to understand the meaning of consecration, we need to study the above referenced verses.

I. THE BASIS OF CONSECRATION

Second Corinthians 5:14-15 clearly shows us that the

constraining power of the Lord's love is the basis for God's children to live unto Him who died for them and has been raised. A man lives unto the Lord because he is constrained by the Lord's love. According to the original language, the word *constrained* can be translated "pressed on from all sides," that is, tightly confined on all sides. It means to be tightly bound and wrapped up. Love has bound us up, and we cannot run away. When a person is in love, he will have a sense of bondage. We are bound by Him; we have no way out. He has died for us, and we should live unto Him today. Hence, love is the basis of consecration. A man consecrates himself to the Lord because of the Lord's love. No one can consecrate himself unless he first touches the Lord's love. A man must touch the Lord's love before he can consecrate himself to Him. When one touches the Lord's love, consecration spontaneously follows.

Consecration is based on the Lord's love. But it is also based on the Lord's right. This is the truth revealed in 1 Corinthians 6:19-20: "You are not your own...For you have been bought with a price." Our Lord gave His own life for us; He even became the ransom to purchase us back to Himself. We are those who are purchased by the Lord. Because the Lord has redeemed us, we willingly lose our own freedom for Him. We are no longer our own; we are the Lord's. We must glorify God in our bodies because we are not our own; we have been bought by the Lord with a price. The blood which the Lord shed on the cross is the price He paid. Therefore, as far as the Lord's right is concerned, we belong to the Lord.

We must be clear that we are those purchased by the Lord. He has purchased us with the highest price. He bought us, not with silver or gold, but with His own blood. Here we see the Lord's love as well as His right. We serve the Lord because He loves us, and we follow Him because He has a right over us. The right secured through redemption constrains us to give ourselves to the Lord. The love that results from redemption also constrains us to give ourselves to Him. The basis of consecration is His right as well as His love. It is a legal right, and it is beyond all human sentimental love.

These are the two reasons that we have to give ourselves to the Lord.

II. THE MEANING OF CONSECRATION

Merely being constrained by love or acknowledging His legal right does not constitute consecration. After a person has been constrained by the Lord's love and has acknowledged His right, there is a further step that he should take. This step will bring him on to a new position. Through the Lord's constraining and based on His purchase, we separate ourselves from every other thing. Henceforth, we live for and unto the Lord. This is consecration. In some instances in the Old Testament, the Chinese Union Version translates the word *consecration* as "the receiving of the holy service." To receive the holy service is to receive the ministry of service to God. This is a holy service. This is consecration. Consecration is receiving the ministry of serving God. It is to say to the Lord, "Today I will separate myself from everything to serve You, because You have loved me."

III. A CONSECRATED PERSON

Let us look at Exodus 28:1-2 and 29:1, 4, 9-10.

After reading these verses, we can see that consecration is a very special matter. The nation of Israel was a nation chosen by God (Exo. 19:5-6), but it did not become a consecrated nation. There were twelve tribes among the Israelites, but not all the twelve tribes received the holy service. The tribe of Levi was one of the twelve tribes. They were a tribe chosen by God (Num. 3:11-13), but they were not a consecrated tribe. Among the many Levites, only the household of Aaron received the holy service. Not all of the Israelites received the holy service, not even all of the Levites. Only the household of Aaron received the holy service. In order to be consecrated, one had to belong to this household. If one were not a member of this household, he could not consecrate himself. Only the members of this household—the household of Aaron—were qualified to be priests, and only they could consecrate themselves.

Thank God, today we are the members of this household.

Those who believe in the Lord are the members of this household. All who have been saved by grace are priests (Rev. 1:5-6). God has chosen us to be the priests. Initially, only the members of Aaron's household could consecrate themselves; if anyone else came near, he would have been put to death (Num. 18:7). We must remember that only those chosen by God to be priests can consecrate themselves. Thus, only the members of this household could consecrate themselves. Today God has chosen us to be the priests; therefore, we are the members of this household. Hence, we are qualified to consecrate ourselves.

Here we see that man does not consecrate himself because he has chosen God. Rather, God is the One who chooses and calls, and then man consecrates himself to Him. Those who consider that they are doing God a favor by forsaking all are but outsiders; they are not consecrated at all. We must realize that our service to God is not a favor or courtesy to God. It is not a matter of offering ourselves to God's work, but a matter of God being gracious to us and giving us a portion of His work. It is God who has given us the glory and the beauty. The Bible tells us that the holy garment of the priest is for glory and beauty (Exo. 28:2). Consecration is God giving us glory and beauty; it is God calling us into His service. If we boast in anything at all, we must boast in our marvelous Lord. There is nothing marvelous for the Lord to have servants like us. The marvelous thing is for us to have such a Lord! We must see that consecration is the result of being chosen. Serving God is an honor to us. We are not uplifting God, as if we were sacrificing anything for Him or as if we had any glory in ourselves. Consecration is God giving us the glory. We should prostrate ourselves before Him and say, "Thank You that I can have a part in Your service. There are so many people in this world, yet I am chosen to have a part in it!" Consecration is our honor, not our sacrifice. It is true that we need to have the greatest sacrifice, but there is no sense of sacrifice in consecration. There is only the full sense of God's glory.

IV. THE WAY OF CONSECRATION

Leviticus 8:14-28 speaks of a bull, two rams, and a basket

of unleavened bread. The bull was for the sin offering; the first ram was for the burnt offering; and the second ram and the basket of unleavened bread were for the consecration offering.

A. The Sin Offering

In order to receive the holy service before God, that is, in order to consecrate oneself to God, the first thing that has to be taken care of is the propitiation for sin. Only a saved person, one who belongs to the Lord, can consecrate himself. The sin offering is the basis of consecration.

B. The Burnt Offering

Following this, we see two rams. We need to study Leviticus 8:18-28 carefully. One ram was for the burnt offering; it was to be burned. The other was for the offering of consecration; it enabled Aaron to serve God.

What is a burnt offering? A burnt offering is an offering which is burned completely. The priest could not eat the flesh of the burnt offering. All the flesh of the burnt offering was burned completely. The problem of our sin is settled by the sin offering, but the burnt offering makes us acceptable to God. The Lord Jesus bore our sins on the cross. This refers to His work as the sin offering. At the same time, while the Lord Jesus was on the cross, the veil was rent from top to bottom, bringing us into the Holy of Holies. This is His work as the burnt offering. The sin offering and the burnt offering start at the same place, but they arrive at different destinations. They start where the sinner is. The sin offering stops at the propitiation of sin, but the burnt offering brings the sinner further by making him acceptable to God. The burnt offering is the offering which makes a sinner acceptable in the Beloved. It goes further than the sin offering. The burnt offering is the sweet savor of the Lord Jesus before God that secures God's acceptance of Him. Today when we offer Him to God, we are accepted by God as well. We are not only forgiven through the sin offering but also accepted through the Lord Jesus.

C. The Offering of Consecration

1. The Sprinkling of the Blood

After the first ram was slain, the second ram followed. What was done with the second ram after it was slain? The first thing that was done was the putting of blood upon the tip of the right ear of Aaron and his sons, upon the thumb of their right hand, and upon the big toe of their right foot. This means that since God has accepted us in Christ, we should acknowledge the blood's separation of our ears, hands, and feet fully unto God. We should declare that our ears, hands, and feet are fully God's. Because of redemption, our ears, which were made for hearing, should now hear for God; our hands, which were made for working, should now work for God. Our legs, which were made for walking, should now walk for God. We apply the blood upon the tip of our right ear, the thumb of our right hand, and the big toe of our right foot. This means that our ears, hands, and feet have all been purchased by the Lord. We should say to the Lord, "Because of Your redemption, Lord, from this day forward, I will no longer consider my two ears to be my own, or my two hands and my two feet to be my own. Because You have redeemed me, Lord, my entire being will henceforth belong to You; it is no longer mine."

Blood is the mark of possession. It is also the symbol of love. Both the "price" spoken of in 1 Corinthians 6 and the "love" spoken of in 2 Corinthians 5 refer to this blood. Because there is blood, love, and possession, our entire being is not our own. The Lord has shed His blood, and we must acknowledge the rightful claim of this blood upon us. Because the Lord loves us, we will confess that our entire being belongs to Him alone.

2. The Wave Offering

After the sprinkling of the blood, there was the wave offering. We must remember that when the second ram was slain, its blood was put on the ear, the thumb, and the toe. This is still not consecration. It is just the basis of consecration. The sprinkling of the blood is merely a confession of love and of right. It qualifies us for consecration, but the actual consecration comes after this.

After the second ram was slain and its blood was sprinkled, the fat and the right shoulder (right thigh) were taken, and out of the basket, an unleavened cake, a cake of oiled bread, and one wafer were also taken. All these things signify the two aspects of the Lord Jesus. The shoulder is the strong part, showing us the divine aspect of the Lord Jesus. Fat is rich, signifying the aspect of God's glory. Bread is of the vegetable life, showing us His highest humanity. He is the perfect man, who is unleavened and unblemished. He is full of the anointing oil, being filled with the Holy Spirit. Like a wafer, His nature, the sentiments in His heart, and His spiritual insight are fine, tender, and fragile, being full of feeling and compassion. All of these things were placed in the hands of Aaron, who took them and waved them before the Lord. After this they were burned with the burning of the burnt offering. This is consecration.

Here we need some explanation. The Hebrew word *consecration* means "to have one's hands filled." Both Darby's translation and Young's concordance refer to this meaning. Initially the hands were empty, now they are filled. When Aaron's hands were filled with so many things, he was filled with the Lord and there was consecration. When Aaron's hands were empty, there was no consecration. When Aaron's hands were filled and his hands could no longer hold anything except the Lord, there was consecration.

What then is consecration? God demanded that the household of Aaron serve Him as priests. But Aaron could not come presumptuously. First, his sins had to be taken care of, and then he had to be accepted in Christ. His hands (denoting work) had to be full of Christ. He had to have nothing but Christ. Only then was there consecration. What is consecration? Simply put, consecration is, as Paul said, "I exhort you therefore, brothers, through the compassions of God to present your bodies a living sacrifice, holy, well pleasing to God, which is your reasonable service" (Rom. 12:1).

Before the Lord, we need to see that in this life there is only one way for us to take, that is, serving God. We have no other way. Serving God is our only way. In order to serve God, we have to present our entire bodies to Him. From this day forward, our ears will listen for the Lord, our hands will work for the Lord, and our feet will run for the Lord. Our two ears will only listen to the Lord's word, our two hands will only do the Lord's work, and our two feet will only walk the way of the Lord. We are here only to serve God. We have consecrated ourselves as an offering, a sacrifice; we have consecrated our all to Him. Furthermore, our two hands will be filled with Christ; they will uplift Him and express Him. This is what consecration is all about. Only when we have done this, will God say, "This is consecration." This saturation of Christ is what God calls consecration.

Consecration means that we have touched the Lord's love and have recognized His right. For these reasons, we can come before God and beg for the privilege to serve. It is not just a matter of God's calling us but of our offering ourselves to serve. We should say, "O God! I am Yours. I have been bought by You. In the past I was under Your table, hoping to eat a little of the fallen bread crumbs, but from this day forward, I want to serve You. Today I choose to serve You. I have been accepted in the Lord. May I also be granted a little portion in the great task of serving You? Be merciful to me so that I can have a part in Your service. In granting salvation to many, You did not pass me by or reject me; You saved me. Now give me a part among the many who serve You; do not reject me."

This is how you present yourself to the Lord. Everything is for Christ and for Him alone. When you present yourself to Him in this way, you have consecration. This is what Romans 12 calls the presenting of our body. Romans 6 speaks of the consecration of the members. This is like the sprinkling of the blood on the ears, the hands, and the feet. Romans 12 speaks of the consecration of the whole body. It is the filling up of both hands with Christ. This links the Old Testament and the New Testament in a perfect way.

V. THE GOAL OF CONSECRATION

The goal of consecration is not to become a preacher for

God or to work for Him. The goal of consecration is to serve Him. The result of consecration is service. In the original language the word *service* means "to wait upon." This means that a person is prepared to serve. We must remember that the goal of consecration is to wait upon God. Waiting upon someone may not be strenuous work. To wait upon God means that you stand when He wants you to stand. If He wants to shuffle you aside, you allow Him to shuffle you aside, and if He wants you to run, you run. This is what it means to wait on Him.

God requires that all Christians offer up their bodies to wait on Him. This does not necessarily mean that He wants you to stand at the pulpit or evangelize some remote land. It means to wait on God. If God sends someone to the pulpit, that person has no choice but to speak. If God sends someone to remote lands, he has no choice but to go. All our time is for God, but the work that we do is flexible. Everyone should wait on God, but the specific work that one should engage in is flexible. We must learn to wait on God. The presenting of one's body is for serving God.

As long as we are Christians, we have to serve God all our lives. As soon as a person consecrates himself, he must realize that from that point on, the Lord's requirement comes first. Service to God becomes one's lifelong mission. May God be gracious to us and show us that our service to Him is our rightful duty. We should show every believer that henceforth we are those who serve the Lord. We must realize that as Christians, we can no longer be loose in anything. I am not saying that we should not be faithful and committed to our career or that we can be idle. This is not what I mean. We still need to be faithful and serious in our vocation. But before God we must see that our entire life is directed towards our service to God. We do everything for the purpose of obeying God's will and pleasing Him. This is the reality of consecration.

Consecration is not how much we can give to God. It is being accepted by God and being granted the honor of serving Him. Consecration is reserved for Christians alone; it is not for everyone. Only the saved ones, those who belong to the

Lord, can consecrate themselves. Consecration means that we say, "Lord, You have given me the opportunity and the right to come before You and to serve You." It is saying, "Lord, I am Yours. My ears were purchased by the blood; they belong to You. My hands were purchased by the blood; they belong to You. My feet were purchased by the blood; they belong to You. From now on I can no longer use them for myself."

We do not beg others to consecrate themselves. Instead, we tell them that a way is now available for them to consecrate themselves. There is a way to serve our God, the Lord of hosts. We must be clear that we are here to serve the Lord of hosts. It is grossly wrong to think that consecration is a matter of granting God a favor.

The revelation in the Old Testament is very clear. A man can only consecrate himself to God under His approval. The New Testament also exhorts us to consecrate ourselves through the compassions of God. God loves us so much; therefore, we have to consecrate ourselves. This is the most reasonable service. This is not a request for favor; this is the most reasonable thing, the most natural thing, to do. Consecration does not depend upon our willingness. It is because of God's abounding grace that we can consecrate ourselves. We must see that having the right to be God's servant is the greatest honor of our life. It is a joyful thing for a man to be saved. It is a far more joyful thing for a man to have a part in God's service! Who do we think our God is? We have to see His greatness and His glory. Only then will we see the tremendous significance and honor of this service! What a tremendous thing it is for us to receive His grace and be counted worthy of serving Him!